Stabs and Fences

Stabs and Fences
and later poems

John Manson

WITH AN INTRODUCTION BY
ALAN RIACH

K&B
Kennedy & Boyd

Kennedy & Boyd
an imprint of
Zeticula Ltd
The Roan
Kilkerran
KA19 8LS
Scotland

www.kennedyandboyd.co.uk
admin@kennedyandboyd.co.uk

First published in 2012

ISBN 978-1-84921-075-1

To the memory of my parents

William Manson 1881-1941
Christina Miller 1900-1977
Crofters

Contents

Sutherland again

Malevich in Edinburgh

from Take Five 2006

Uncollected

Stabs and Fences: An Introduction to John Manson

John Manson is a poet of rare integrity and distinction. This is a deeply impressive collection of lean, durable poems as firm in their positioning and place as the necessary stabs and fences required on croft or smallholding. When so much of the world is given over to the venality of celebrity-culture with all its superficiality and distractions, work of this kind is apt to be undervalued or overlooked entirely. Here there is a gathering of decades, spanning a writing life over more than half a century and crossing the whole stretch of Scotland, from Sutherland to the Stewartry of Kirkcudbright. And there is a continuity, a sense of character, at the heart of the thing, a compassionate and questioning sensibility, coming through tragedies, loss, maturing into wisdom, quietly pronouncing utter condemnation upon those people and things that work to limit comprehension and stifle human potential.

These poems start from personal experience, self-knowledge and mature understanding, but their concern is always outward, connecting people across differences in a vision that offers hope for justice in society. These are not the poems of a young man. When they confront the inimical, narrowing forces that impinge upon us all, they are confrontational in the best way: they will not permit our forgiveness or tolerance of people and acts that should and must be opposed. They embody what Seamus Heaney called the redress of poetry. This is one of the most necessary books of its time.

The poems seem spare, keen, brief and to the point, but the small-press publications from which they are collected range across time and occasion. The beginning is in ancestry, both family and economic history. The work of crofting, both violent and tender, imbues the lives of working people with their own controlled and liberating character. From the first poems, the energies at war between a desire for self-expression and the enforcement of conformity is fierce. Memorials to the dead evoke this for the living, challenge our indifference, resist the banal mollification of ignorance or obfuscation.

Noting a historian's reference to a period of 'social tension and upheaval', the poet asks whether this might be a reference to the Highland Clearances. The even tone of the question masks the force behind the words, a kind of rage – and the mask of simple words and phrases both covers the ferocity and allows it a controlled expression, articulate incredulity at the inhumanity of the landowners and their factors and the poet's sustained exclamation of protest. The banality of violent eviction, the subtle educational procedure that helps with public coercion and the cover-up of how the stories are told by the officials, all are implied, accurately noted and quietly condemned by the poems, while the language remains level, calm, judicious and patient. When Manson describes a ruined wooden window's lintel on which a skelf – a splinter or shard of wood – 'tilts / like a balance' – you know you're in good hands. Every word seems to carry multiple meanings and tones – simple words like 'echo' or 'Works' and phrases like 'It's of no interest to anyone' or 'There are no vandals' – are infinitely delicate in suggestion of tone and meaning. Loss, abandonment, distortion of presence, an understanding of acceptance and protest, knowing one has to go on and knowing equally that due time must be given for lament and appraisal of what has been lost, and deepening understanding that the injustices that continue to bring such devastation to people require an opposition and resistance – all these are active in the poems. They are unobtrusive but adamantine. As Iain Crichton Smith once put it: 'They seem to me, in the main, excellent thoughtful poems and in their attacks on dogma very heartening.'

Again and again, there are signs of personal, autobiographical resonance, a trace that something has arisen from lived experience – but there is never a sense of self-indulgence, emotional excess, sentimental sorrowing. The ironies are shrewdly maintained. Surely things have moved on from the eighteenth and nineteenth centuries; surely, here in the new millennium, we have no need to be reminded of the assumptions of class prejudice, and yet, when the Colonel and his wife drive by in their Land Rover they are still the objects of deference, and even if, unlike their ancestors, they speak to their neighbours, nevertheless the Hall is still 'six times the size of any croft'. What remains of value is to be understood in the world of living creatures, and it is no diminishment but rather an illumination that an old ewe and an old woman might equally have a 'stock of lore' dismissed and destroyed: 'Where to lie on wet nights / How to scaff for pellets' but it is certainly an oppression that a human being might be forced to be like 'a stab [a post] in a fence': 'sawed to size' and constrained by the wire.

It is a draught of cold water to read love poems of loss, where the poet has no recourse to appeal or hope for remittance. We recognise the truth in some things that are difficult, things which our current mass media never deal with: 'Love is a ring / Love is a scar' – what television programme could express that truth in fairness? When an image of delight appears, the appetite for its unexpected brightness or absurdity or historical fashion makes it leap: someone comes into a poem in 'a dress of polka dots' or 'in a white suit / like a crocus'. How bright such pictures are, in a life – the life of any one of us – which might value them truly. How honest is the understanding in lines like those that open 'Do Not Tell Me': 'I knew you were strong and real / knew you would not be loyal'. R.D. Laing would have admired the emotional and intellectual perceptiveness that opens the self with a metaphorical scalpel and sees that the beloved 'lied knowing' that the jealous lover's 'guilt at being jealous' would make him 'accept the lie' and yet still leave him with the question, 'Did you lie?'

But the personal and universal experiences in the love poems are tempered and balanced by the geographical locations the poems evoke. In Fife, in Edinburgh, in Kirkpatrick Durham near Dumfries, the necessary facts of work and domesticity, of friendships, family and time, all build slowly and separately into a monument of lasting provocation. We must not think ourselves superior to anyone, for anyone has a human potential that no world can ever completely fulfil, but we must not think ourselves destined for nothing better: conditions can be and should be improved and anyone can help in such work, if the knowledge is shared. When Manson finds some old notes made as a young man when a young woman came to see him, his old Scots voice reflects:

The feelins ir the same
Nae mair mature
Tho I'm mair mature

And this suggests the quality of humour that connects his emotional intensity of presence with anyone willing to read sympathetically, not to caricature what might easily be mocked but to give the poems the patience their author has given his readers.

A remarkable sequence of poems is prompted by an exhibition of the Russian avant-garde painter Kasimir Malevich in Edinburgh in 1993. Following John Berger's seminal book, *Success and Failure of Picasso*, Manson in 'The Moment of Cubism' asks the necessary question of modern art and the modern world – technological advances may make significant difference in social and aesthetic terms, but what of those people to whom the Eiffel Tower, electric light and aeroplanes mean nothing? Malevich is perhaps most famous for his painting 'Black Square'. In reproductions, the painting is pretty much exactly as its title describes but to make the journey to see it in itself, without the aid of mechanical reproduction, involves work, risk and personal investment. The New Zealand poet Gregory O'Brien recently did this and reported back in his book, *Beauties of the octagonal pool* (2012) that it appears 'much less absolute in real life'. It 'looks as though it must have spent the past eighty years stashed behind a filing cabinet... Far from the pristine, resolute painting encountered in books, the canvas resembles a segment of the Russian steppes viewed from an aeroplane: all cracks and rivers and flooded valleys, moonlit.'

It is as if the painting has matured, an ancient work of the then avant-garde, weathered into a new meaning. Similarly, in John Manson's poems, the conviction is constant as the human agent grows deeper and more lined with understanding. The value of lived experience in the actual world cannot be transmitted through simulacra – the work of art in the age of mechanical reproduction cannot be exactly reproduced – unless that quality of life comes through, in texture, time and tension. Maybe poems can do this more readily than pictures, because words carry the nuances of meaning whereas the material facts of canvas and paint convey something else and require a physical presence. So John Manson's poems enter that tangible immediacy as you read them, and this book allows them, finally, to be given to your eyes.

And to be heard. For the sounds of the poems matter, in English and in Scots. The voices they carry are literally from the past, vocabulary and expressions that come directly from particular regions and places in Scotland, as well as from the international currency of English in which Manson has been a masterly reader and translator of poetry from other languages for many years. Influences are evident from Bertolt Brecht, Eugenio Montale, Pablo Neruda, Fernando Pessoa and others – there is no narrowness or insularity in his reading. Yet the limitations of any single life define it, just as an openness to experience and literature enable it. All John Manson's poems proceed from this.

The Scots-language poems describing the work of the crofter are as intimate with the hard details of the economy of that world as the English-language poems are assured in their reference and speculative balance. A spoken gesture of support, of human contact, engenders a moment of doubt in the poem 'At The Edinburgh Book Festival, 2001', as the poet recognises the liability of trying to be friendly in a world of political suspicion and uncertainty. In 'Susan Weissman – Victor Serge: The Course Is Set On Hope', a reading of a book which appears to be historically objective and thorough asks a simple question about the ideology that underpins its conclusion: 'After 1918 the Party got almost nothing right anywhere / However one man got almost everything right everywhere'. Manson thus exposes the bias at the heart of individualism and highlights the much-denigrated value of the work of socialism. In his poem for James Leslie Mitchell (Lewis Grassic Gibbon), the full significance of what might otherwise have seemed merely platitude is immense: '*The body is dead, but the spirit will remain / The work that he has done will remain...*' However, against that we must look at the Scottish National War Memorial, when words from Grassic Gibbon's *Sunset Song* might alert us immediately to the duplicity of the wording on the memorial referring to the soldiers shot for desertion in the First World War.

The final section of hitherto uncollected poems brings further pleasures of humour and comradeship, condemnation and scorn. The 'Laird and Tall Woman' still travel 'business class' but a Goth, in a 'Marcel Marceau mask / seal's eyelashes / and bat's gloves', across fifty years of difference in age, still allows the recognition of affinity and friendliness: 'we were both wearing black coats'. In 'Gordon Brown's Schooldays' as vicious a Rector as you'll find in any fiction invites those schoolboys keen to watch a football game to visit him in his office, which they do, only to find it was a trap: 'he got them in one by one, gave them a good belting, and told them if they tried to play truant that afternoon, they'd get another belting every day for a month.' Manson's judgement is implacable and fine:

> The language of power
> The language of terror
>
> A thrashing for thinking
>
> May *his* hands burn in hell

But even so, it is not only the force of condemnation even in a poem as focused as this that remains from reading the book as a whole, but rather the sense that we all have the need to be in connection, and the isolation our world sets us into will never be enough for this basic human desire, to recognise our solitude and work in our companionship. Or as John Manson puts it, in 'In St David's Street':

> I wanted to speak to you
> And you to speak to me

In the end what we have is a collection of poems that delivers a whole sensibility, a solitary, companionable man who values the achievements and the aspirations of great art, the need for accessible education, the struggle for social justice and egalitarianism, and whose poems speak decisively of these things to all, with neither exclusivity nor excuse. The heroes and heroines of labour are as real as those who drove the tanks at Stalingrad, and the poets and artists whose work really helps us to live are of their company. John Manson is of their company. And there is no exemption by privilege of class, wealth or birth, in the courts of life and art and morning. And there is no hesitation in this work of affirmation.

Alan Riach
Scottish Literature
Glasgow University

Sutherland

To An Unconceived Child

'My personality was crushed gradually, but surely, and an imitation of life grew out like
    a derision of everything which was sacred to me...'
(N.M. Seedo, *In the Beginning Was Fear*)

On a night of wind and rain
The crofter used to hope
The lambs would 'stay where they were'

Stay where *you* are
In the egg
In the seed unmet
Until I am sure
You will never know
The debilitation of sin
Or the holiness of salvation

Or stagger without sound
In slow motion
From the gas chamber of prayer
Lethal to life
As a stunned fly
Drags his legs away
To a dark corner
No one looks by

Or live in the head
Live to work
Liking in nothing
Owning in the name of loving
An iron implement
Shouting psalms

The aamel wags at the tail o the plou
The horses pu on the chains
I to the hills will lift mine eyes

What language did I learn
On the Bass Rock
Of a Caithness croft

Among the yithings and the soughings
The subserviences
The shutting up
It was reported he spoke good Calvinese

The mear's lips
In the gowden sun

The act a thousand times hated once admitted
White seed spurting on white frost

The stirk's on his tether
And his baakie's doon

The hobbled horse
The coo in the branks
The yowe in her hems
The high jumper shackled

I am the seed under the stone
I am the tree that grew out of the wall
        the spider that never reached the beam
        the stream that sometimes cracks the surface

The gress growes up
Around the stane
Bit in the mool
White ruit
Yella shuit

Christ wis lucky efter aa
Some ane rowed the stane awa

Here guilt is with the innocent, the sacrificer is the sacrificed...' (Joszef Lengyel, *The Spell*)

This is it then
We cannot annul

Let the demanders
Emotional blackmailers
And manipulators note
They told us it was right
It was right for themselves
And they won as they intended

Stay where you are
Until I am sure
You will never know
The suspicion of a repressive woman
The distortion of placation
(In emotion, too, exploitation
Leads only to impoverishment)
The blame of your wrecker
A victim's conscience
The liberal who thinks
You may not be entirely to blame
The socialist who thinks
His understanding will surely make you conform

Conformism, keep it

aamel - swingle-tree;
yithings - lispings of 'yes';
baakie - iron spike for tethering an animal;
branks - a kind of bridle or halter with wooden side-pieces;
hems - triangle (in the case of sheep)

A Farewell To Anarchism

We cannot change the views we held in the past and we must never forget them or the origins which gave rise to them. But can we not begin to change the views we hold today? Should we not leave our isolated nests, our superiority complexes, created only by our difficulties? Should we not crush the extravagances of our rebellion, of our feelings of oppression, to rejoin the others, not to be complacent, but to show the basic causes of our difficulties, the same as those of thousands of other people?

At St. Andrew's, Golspie

I tread on rows of thick flat red slabs,
Scuffing over the hay with my foot.
Many are plain; some might have been scratched by a nail.
Initials, names, dates—

This Beureal Pleas belongs to John Sothrland, 1731.[1]
A half-drawn margin without legend.
A border inscribed on the level part of a field.

Cruciform kirk, tide-marked harling,
Bare surrounds of windows, gables, eaves, doors.
I press down the tongue of the sneck.
The stalls have been scrubbed with light grey paint.

The Sutherland loft cost *Fourty one pd. three Shill & Sevenpence, 1739.*[2]
Initials, Arms, Sans Peur; worm-drilled varnish.
I climb the outside stair, not for the ordinary,
Rusting footscraper on either side. Locked.

Who sat in it? The Roman senator
On a red plinth on Beinn a' Bhraghaidh?
The historian says 'The transformation in agriculture...
Was not without a corresponding period
Of social tension and upheaval.'[3]
Did he mean the Highland Clearances?

---

[1]   This inscription is in the Kirkton yard at Kirkton farm.
[2]   *St. Andrew's, Golspie* (Congregational Board, n.d.).
[3]   *Dunrobin Castle* (Guide Book, text by R.J. Adam).

At A Ruined Croft
Cnoc Bad a' Chrasgaith

The walls are down to window height
        battlemented
In the wind the skelf of a lintel tilts
        like a balance

Just a piece of stick
In a year — or ten — one end will wear away
And it will fall
It's of no interest to anyone
There are no vandals
No one has bothered to derange it

The trees wave their besoms on the ridge
There is an echo of wind
The drills in the field stay in their corrugations

And at the east gable
A corroded pipe — one in a hill of 500 acres —
Works

Crofter

I

I hung that gate
I laid that pipe
I built that barn
I felled that tree
I cut that divot
I shot that stag

II

Without doubt his products, a few sheep and cattle,
Were part of the process of alienation
When they were sold on the free, unplanned market.
Much more profound was the self-alienation
Of all his feelings away from human beings
To land, implements, materials, animals.

Ill LAST CEILIDH

I went over in the glooming
Soon after I heard he was home.
He sat in his old chair
Along the wall from the window.

I did not see his hand shake
And his word was as strong as ever;
An old letter from Red River,
The duel with the deer.

The Value Of A Man

If you do not want to think, say
He was always a bit that way.

Yes, he was simple.
But once he had a place.

The agent offered credit,
Saw he had stock,
And they rouped the stock
To pay the bill.

The strong men use him now
At sale days, dipping or threshing.

He thinks he owns all the farms of the strath
And in their meritocratic way
The neighbours do not forget to ask him
About the crops and the animals.

I have heard them
In the shop, in the Post Office,
Making a fool
Of the fool.

If a man is simple,
Let him be simple.

The shepherd seeks the one which is lost.
A man has no value.

(The agent kept his job.
The firm stayed in business.)

Colonel And Mrs

Colonel and Mrs wave from their Land Rover.
'A fine man.' 'She's very nice.'
The bells are silent in the Old Lodge
But the Hall is six times the size of any croft,
The farm steading wired for deep litter.
Colonel and Mrs are not like their kind.
They speak to their neighbours.
They may be genuinely helpful.
We do not want to be ungrateful.
But they remain Colonel and Mrs.
They are sure of their roles
Among the stooks and the coles.
They ask the questions
And we answer them.

— We're all equal before the Lord
But when we get to heaven
Too bad if we find
They're Colonel and Mrs there too.
The Lord hadn't the heart to declass them.

Jean

The old woman lived alone on her croft in winter
As long as she could look after herself.
She went to the October sale
And died next February.

She had a cold and went to bed.
She was not missed from the door.
Water stayed in the well,
Coal at the end of the road.
The vans did not go up.
The bottle did for a day.

The hospital was the best place.
She was far gone by then.
They don't last long there.
The funeral was big.
She was saved.
She was a card.

Bremner

No one has seen his hand.*
He walks on the toe of a built-up boot,
His knee knifed out.

Machinery took his orra jobs.
Rolling fleeces, feeding hens.

Middle-aged in the Old Folk's Home,
He is the messenger
— A job he protects by fist and temper.

*with acknowledgements to my mother

Robert And Elizabeth

She was three, he was five
When their mother died.
Brought up by an aunt,
They never married.

I met then in the Home —
Parcels re-addressed from the convalescent hospital.
No one knew them in their young days here.
They have always been as they are.

But I suppose she kept the house
And he settled there when his seafaring days were over.
Now at the age of eighty-four,
He takes her in tow across the floor.

Old Baby (1)

I drove them to the hill every evening
A score of ewes
The grandmother of the flock
Old Baby
Did not want to go
She'd double-back half-way there
Or wander off in another direction

If I let her off
Some of the others would do the same
So I made her go
Though her sides had holes like a starving cow

But she was right
I saw it wasn't perversity
When she had triplets – all dead –
At the age of nine

Old Baby (2)

So old Baby had to go to the ring too
The flock had to be sold
The first time off the land
She was bred on
Who should have gone back into it
In a hole dug in soft ground

Now the stock of lore in the sawn-off head was useless
Where to lie on wet nights
How to scaff for pellets
Just one of the others
The oldest, the shabbiest

A Stab In A Fence

A stab may be four inches square
And up to six feet or over
It is dead now and sawed to size
It is driven into earth and stones
Wire is strained to the stab
It stands for forty years
Then the yellow wood is grey
The wire hangs red and broken
A man is not a stab in a fence
He is made into one

Old Stab

The wood wears a grey skin
Lichen seals the ridges of fibres
The head is a ruin
Of concentric amphitheatres

The Tree In The Wall

A tree grew out of the wall
About two feet above the ground.
A seed must have lodged
On a moss-grown ledge
Or been put in with the mud
With which the wall was packed.
It was a birch,
Skin like an onion.
It grew out and up like a pipe
To take smoke over a roof.
They sawed it down
Like a leg below the knee.
But the stump still stands,
Curled up,
Tattered green leaves on the twigs.

What Is She Reading Now?
A dream

I meet the post down the brae
Turn back and you're coming

I tear into your parcel
Jealous of your books
Knots and folds hold me back
I know there's no excuse

And they're only yellow Penguins
Thick edges of old mustard
Bunches of glue-glazed signatures
Burst away from the backs

You take the parcel from me
You do not seem to notice

Robbie's Kist

Sorry, Robbie, I left your kist behind
On the damp floorboards under flaking distemper.
It made the first flitting from Caithness to Sutherland
But not to the new house in Edinburgh.

It was the kist where the cat had kittens
On a *News of the World* in which Hammond made a double century.
I knew the blood stains were no longer there
But somehow hoped to find the chandlers' accounts
Cleared out sometime somewhere on the way.
The boat took it all, I heard it said.

It was the kist that bade in the attic
In the mythical days of the herring fishing from Wick.
You never went back to the sea after the War
And 1941 was not so long after 1914.

— Why do I worry about your old kist?
Your last kist is rotting in the kirkyard at Canisbay
And you inside it.

A sequence

In The Present

I did not know you
You did not know me
Yet it was right
It was in the present
Not asking a question
Nor making a promise
You asked nothing
You had no need
You had secrets
Too hard to tell
You did not drive my head
Into a shell
Love is a ring
Love is a scar

August

In the hot days, we played
In tired heat, we parted

I am back, and the night
Cools now and darkens

The door is open and empty
But you are inside...

Cool too...never so cool
In a dress of polka dots

You Are The Same

'... altro tempo frastorna
la tua memoria...'
- Eugenio Montale, 'La casa dei doganieri'

It is always the same
As the last time
The force of circumstance
Did not win
Though I walk backwards
Down the road from you

You are the same
And I remember
Time did not cancel
Another time
We go on living
For a little while

April

Snow fell from the sun
The sun hovered, diffident

March was black frost, east wind
Earth pitted iron

Did you leave?
Did the bus stick?
Did you take the train?

Suddenly
I met you
In your white suit
Like a crocus

Do Not Tell Me

I knew you were strong and real
  knew you would not be loyal

Once we blew
A bubble of glass
That was our room
We lived in it

Do not tell me
What the eye did not see

(I know you made a time
To speak your mind)

Drunk tired ebb tide
Rocks rising

You branded me with words
As if you were quoting

Did You Lie?

I had a right to be jealous
I had something to be jealous of
Though you attacked me for believing it
Said there was nothing in it
And you lied knowing
That my guilt at being jealous
Would make me accept the lie
Did you lie?

Old Photos

None of them is like you
I try to make one
I like to think one shows you
As I wish you had been
No, as you were almost
If I could think back
Behind the avalanche
But this is gawkish
And this is too dark
Can I look at them?
Can I look at you?

Fife

In Crombie Again

I

We were late in leaving Aberdour
where we missed the tide to Inchcolm
No one had bothered to look it up
Now in a minibus with strange colleagues
we are driving fast through the ancient lands of Crombie
part of the shire of Culross, in stooks again
trying to catch up the time
to spend an educational half-hour in Culross
half an hour in Culross
where every stone has a history
We are driving above Limekilns
the Gellet Rock, the King's Cellars, the Ghauts
We are driving above Charlestown
the planned village, the sutlery, the kilns, the caves
We are driving above Crombie kirk, point, place, pier

II

Not so in the autumn three years earlier
When we were getting to know each other
Meeting by accident, wilful accident
Nervous arrangements
On our best behaviour
Feeling our way

Heat out of the day
The ripening of growth
Taking in the corn
The thresh of sheaves forked on the load
Now the hum of the motor

Shiver in the air
Shiver in me

To Crombie Kirk

Another Sunday two years ago
On the other side of the Forth...

We had planned to go to Crombie Kirk
Navigating the pock-marked track
In the lee of the high dyke
Between the estate and Torrie Bay
Past the witch's grave on the foreshore
Ring-holder set in lead
And up the Windmill Brae to see

The fourteenth-century cross in relief
Like a ship's wheel on a chunk of undressed stone
The Latin slab bruised and lichened, fractured and jointed
The aumrie like a niche in a byre for cattle combs
The sextant like a scythe
The spade like a tuskar shaft
The crown and hammer scoured to a face of yellow sand

It made no sense (to anyone else)
To watch at your window
Each fill of black grey cumulus
Mount like an explosion or a fire
Batter its rain into the river
Drain to a chill blue
And hope each one would be the last
I had to go with you to-day

And So We Sat On

And so we sat on
We drew to the fire
The coals were like black crabs
With red bellies
I poked them onto their backs
And their fire went out

Your hair falling over your face
Like the veil of a web
And your hands parting it
Kissing your wind-chapped lips
Your face dissolving
And you shivering in your jeans and cardigan

A Success

He said he'd been overdoing it.
Cancer of the spine.
I'd met him twelve years before
When he was still at school.
He was an outstanding success
And I, the reverse,
Did not want to speak
Even to a dying man.
What should I have said
To a man who would soon be dead?

The Lord's Will

It was the will of the Lord, the Headmistress said,
That throwing the cricket ball had to be cancelled,
And Lindsay, who had injured his hand,
Would not be handicapped in the championship.
A simple faith.

Too bad, Elaine.
He didn't hear you.
You died at thirteen of leukemia
Not drugged by dope and fairy tales
But screaming
I DO NOT WANT TO DIE

Staff-Room Problem

They might be waiting for the bad news at Aberfan
Or embalmed by the lava at Herculaneum.

Tired housewives ballasted by their shopping
In an arc they pose their worry
Over a colleague's respectable problem.

Colleague

He has found a good poem —
He thinks — in a paper.
He passes it to me.
To see if I'll like it?

No. He likes himself
For finding a poem good
After such a long time.
How does he show it?

He leads with his jaw.
His mouth is a box.
He revels in declaration.
He's at the height of a row.

What's he doing though?
Miscalling another poem.

Sutherland again

i.m. My Mother, Christina Miller

1.
The last step was hard
The door half-open
You held the jamb
And the shut edge

Your face contracted
But then it was over
And you were out
Leaving a house behind

2.
And when you are no longer able to look after yourself
You shall be taken to a place of public death

3.
You had your life there
Forgotten, rediscovered
Reticences
Long waits
Yet once I heard your voice stronger in the sitting-room
When you were giving your opinion to the other residents

And I in the outside world
In Edinburgh, Fife, Kirkpatrick Durham
Moving digs and houses
Changing jobs
Writing articles and poems
Making love
Having a child

4.
It's always been hard to tell you
Like *I'm taking six plucking hens to Mrs Campbell's*
And you flushed deep down into your wattles
It's no easier at forty

5.
I am angry now at our honesty
Like reporting the age of three auld yowes
For the Hill Sheep Subsidy

6.
So I went wilfully away
At the end of that last time-table
You didn't see the bairn that time
And there wasn't another time

7.
I was in my usual state of unpreparedness
Well we never went anywhere, did we?
There was always the animals to look after
And who could afford to pay for that?

8.
It ended here
In one way
Written in a ledger
With an iron pen
Among files and packing cases
By a part-time registrar (after 4 p.m.)
Cashier in the grocer's
And he chatting quietly
About his wife's death
She did not go back to Caithness, either

9.
Fresh December day
In open wather
Oor fang cerried on aheid
We scrunched on the mittle
Juist owre the broo o the brae
An facan Little Rogart
Til the nerra troch
Owrehung wi fause gress
Oot o yir hoose noo aa richt
And dumped in a weet holl

10.
You came to my door
In the middle of the night
At first I thought you were a neighbour
But the rubbing came clearer

You wore my old green jacket
Tied with binder twine
Your teeth are here
Your lips are sealed

How did you find your way
This far south in Scotland?
Not in a car for nine years,
A train for twenty two

11.
A phone call in the middle of the afternoon
    But they had rung off
A nail driven into four annual rings

I was on holiday at the time
    A long holiday from home
But I had not written
    After all these years
At twice or thrice a week

Were you still managing on your own?
Were the neighbours looking after you?
Were you still alive?

26.9.81

12 As She Passes

'When I am sitting at the window,
Through the panes, which the snow blurs,
I think I see the image, hers,
That's not now passing ... not passing by ...'
- Fernando Pessoa, 'As She Passes'.

When they're looking out the window
On the slab where you fell that night
- The end of our old life -
The strangers tell me
They think they see your image, yours,
Passing to the well
Which I'm too far away to see
Or think I see.

Malevich in Edinburgh

Auld Notes

Auld notes
I've fund ye agane
Made bi a loun
Whan a lassie cam til see him

And ye've lain throu the year
And traivelled throu the land
In the pages o a buik
I wis readan at the time

The feelins ir the same
Nae mair mature
Tho I'm mair mature

* * *

The third nicht
As we stude
In the lee
0 the skroo
I pu'd ye out
In frunt o me

Syne a nakit lass
In the len-tee
A nakit lass
In the ben-end

Bit wis this no
Owre eisy?
Wir we in luve?
'Let's not bother
About semantics'
Ye said

I didna ken
I lat ye gang
Ye ne'er cam back

Bit did ye e'er gang?
Til me - no
Til ye - ye maun hae dune
Did ye?

loun, lad; skroo, cornstack; len-tee, lean-to; ben-end, best room

Lamban

A slap in the dyk
Nae gate or jambs
Stanes owretapped bi winnelstraes
An auld gairden shilled oot o the rock behint
Twa rhubarb ruits a birk
A yowe strakkit oot lamban bleitan

It wis lee the nicht
Skookan behint the grey-bairdit rickle o stanes
To mak siccar the bag burst
And no lat her ken I wis there

Though the fan o the wund
Thuddit aff the grand
Ye wudna been cauld

slap, gap; dyk, dyke; winnelstraes, withered stems; birk, birch; yowe, ewe; strakkit,
   stretched; bleitan, bleating; skookan, hiding; siccar, sure

At The Curling Pond Shed - A Dream

The ins and outs hae aa faded
I ken I wis wi ye agane

I heerd yir vyce rise and faa
Shaal watter owre slack stanes

      The waal in the side o the brae
      Washed out wi burn watter
      The flagstane slate wi the slide
                O green algae

Ye sat in a bunch o blue faulds
And I in roch dungarees

Bit wha ye wir wi
Or trysted tae
Or hoo we cam back at aa
Or gin ye gaed bifore the daa .. .

The curling stanes ir gane
The waas rot at the found

vyce, voice; shaal, shallow; waal, well; trysted, committed; waas, walls; found,
    foundations

*The next seven poems form a sequence inspired by some of the oilpaintings of
Kasimir Malevich in the Exhibition 'Russian Painting of the Avant Garde
1906-1924' at the Scottish National Gallery of Modern Art, 1993.*

The Scyther (1912)

Malevich, whit wir ye thinkan about?
Can ye see him binnan a shaef
Or biggan a skroo? -
Yin abject peasant in airmour?
He is airmour near eneuch
Lek the bled o his scy,
Trousers lek cylinders
And a lampshade round his middle.
Did he hiv bare feet on the stibble?

binnan a shaef, binding a sheaf; biggan, building; scy, scythe

The Carpenter (1928-32)

And the jiner's airmour
Steel leigs and airms
Buits and apren
Kaleidoscope o grey blue black

Exe in his richt haun
Nail in his left
Is he an exe?
A sneck in a loug
Steel ban across his mou
Reid baird hingan doun bilow
Reid hauns and feice

sneck in a loug, notch in a log; ban, band; mou, mouth

The Reaping Woman (1912)

Gauguin on the steppes

She ees a staak
A Léger cylinder
Sets her heuk til't

Lang clout wipped round her
Wi a tyal
Claes til cuver the bodie
No til shaw't
The wemen in perticular

And yit the shuit's no oonlek
The histry buik picter
Frae the British Museum

The brat wis made out o hessian seck
In ma mither's day
Bit the colour wisna the same
As in the South Seas

ees, eyes; staak, stalk; heuk, hook (sickle); clout, cloth; tyal, cord; shuit, position; brat, apron

Woman with a Rake (1928-1932)

fu o oonrael colour
ovoid heid
splet bleck and white
skirt
bleck and white
airms
ane bleck and ane white
wyst
green and yalla
glivs
ane yalla and ane reid
cuffs
daurk blue and licht blue
buits
ane reid and ane blue
turned out lek a bairn's drawin

ye staun wi yer back
til a raw o houses
lek the lums o a liner
haudan a thin white rake
wi ten white teeth on a grun
o reid bleck white green pink yalla rigs

Mither
ye niver haed time
til staun wi yer back
til the Pentland Firth
wi drifters passan
bitween Strouma island
and the mainland

wearan a coorse brat
ye delled raws o tatties —
their shaws dowed -
wi a fower-prounged graip

on sodden grun
and waited for the trailer
til tak the bags back
til the auld hous

and I'd be coman
up the Back Brench
frae Thirsa Schuil
efter lernan Latin

Peasant Woman (1928-32)

White jaicket wi a collar toucht in
Lang white skirt
A surgeon
A Baptist

Heid splet lek an ovoid
Back o the skull left
Front aa bleck

Bleck hauns and neck
Bleck feet turned out
Lek a bairn's drawin

The Moment Of Cubism[1]

Whit did they ken
O the Tour Eiffel
Electric licht
Or aeroplane flicht?

[1] John Berger, *The Success and Failure of Picasso* (Penguin, 1965, 47-64) defines 'the moment of cubism' as being between 1907 and 1914.

Malevich's Hairst
(cf. *Corn Harvest*, 1565)

Breughel binnan
Aa that's missan
Here is Burns' weary flingan-tree

hairst, harvest; flingan-tree, flail

Gell

The gell splet the skroo
On its steddle
On the heicht
O the brae

Tirlan owre yella strae
Eftir yella strae
Abune the broon strumps
Net lowsed
Frae its nievefus o rips

We held on
Braithless
Wurds swupped
Oot o wir mouths

A tant nicht

gell, gale; steddle, foundation; tirlan, flicking; strumps, ends of stalks; lowsed, loosened;
    nievefus o rips, fistfuls of stalks; swupped, swept; tant, gusty

Loddan Neeps

eftir the photie, 'Among the Turnips' bi Frank Meadow Sutcliffe, Whitby

Torsos o neeps shawed bi the docker
Lig in twa strecht raws
Hinted in frae ither dreels
Box-cairt in bitween
Shale-wings up

Twa horses pu'd up
Ane in the shafts
Ane in side-rips aheid
Aa in sepia sheda

Pints o hems
Pints o lugs

loddan neeps, loading turnips; shawed, with shaws (shows) cut off: docker, cutter; lig,
   lie; raws, rows; hinted, thrown; dreels, drills; shale-wings, shelves which fitted into
   metal sockets on the sides of the box-cart; side-rips, small chains or side ropes; pints
   o hems, points of the two metal bars which go along the edges of the collar; pints o
   lugs, points of ears

Pleuan

The pair snarl and pull
Faem flies aff the bits
The maas cut it fine
And settle in behind
The coulter tears
Siller gress and stibble
And the shinin soc scrapes
Owre stons and worms
The moulboord slicks the cley
The stilts haul the man
Reins wipped round his wrists
He stamps doun the fur
Wi his richt fuit as he gangs

pleuan, ploughing; faem, foam; maas, gulls; siller, silver; soc, ploughshare; moulboord,
    mouldboard; stilts, plough handles; fur, furrow

The Stirk

Aince I sat
On a stirk's heid
And if I hadna
Anither wu'd

Wippled wi rope
He'd been thrown
Re-clamsed
At a year auld

Cords crushed
Throu skin and vein
Cords crushed
Throu flesh and bluid

For days eftir
He stude in his sta
Black bag swelled
Lek a weet battery

re-clamsed, re-use of clamp for crushing testicle cords

Absentee Crofter

So I bigged up the waa
And hollowed out the grun bilow
To haud back the beas
Frae rivan rips
Out o the skroos
Pit out the yowes and lambs
In the mornin at the lambin
Bifore gaan back til wark
In Aiberdeen or Embro

Bit some jobs were niver dune
The midden wis niver pit out
It sank bilow nettles
White Moo's staa wis niver pit richt
She ligged in her ain sharn
The rousted scy blades
Still lig on the bink
And ilka job weill kent brocht up
The hameseeckness o wir ain failyier

beas, beasts; rivan, tugging; sharn, loose dung; rousted, rusted; bink, ledge; ilka, every

Reidhmásach

mindan ma mither

Aff the evenin train
Hotteran awa at Rogart station

I c'ud see the teeter
Bobban doun the brae

Coman near the gate
We swapped shouts
I expect ye'd heerd ma feet

Sae we wir meetan agane
Coman on the past
Lek a bundle
O auld letters

A green year
The beas still out
Snortan and chowan
Blown owre the back
Rivan rank gress
Lyan pu'd up bi the ruits
In the munelicht
Bitween the gavel end
And the barn

mindan, remembering; teeter, hand-held cycle lamp; rivan, tearing; gavel, gable

Yir Brither Wis Lost At Sea
(Suggested by *Xenia* 1, 13 - Eugenio Montale)

Yir brither wis lost at sea;
Ye wir the solemn-lookan mither
At ma back in the snap
The year eftir ma faither deed.
Wearan a white jersey,
Ye didna come out vera weel.

He was a failyier, yir brither.
He'd TB aa richt
Bit did he need til play tennis?

'He cam hom on a stick',
Ye threipit at me, mebbe thinkan,
'And ye'll come hom on a stick.
He'd a lend o money
And niver peyed it back.
He pleu'd sax year fir his brose
And his faither wis haurd on'm.
He'd a pound til gang til Weeck
And naethin whan he cam back.
Aa he tried turned til watter,' mebbe thinkan '
And aa ye try'll turn til watter tae.'

Ah stuck up for'm
Bit did Ah iver see'm?
Ah hae anither snap -
Daith's teeth in a baird in naval uniform.
Mebbe Ah copied him aince
Whan Ah s'udna.
Ah mind o'm frae yir threipins.
Luve growes frae anither's self-alienation.

Ina Manson (1861-1936) is shown with her mother Minnie Campbell (1816 –1910), from David Craig's book *On the Crofters' Trail*, London, 1990.

Ena's

The auld hous wis Ena's.
Bit wha wis Ena?
And whit cam at her?
She deed at seeventy-five
Whan Ah wis fower.

Ah niver askit
And Ah niver heerd tell
O onything she ivir said or did.
At saxty-sax
Ah hae juist warkit oot
She wis ma grand-aunt.

i.m. Ian M. Grant

d. 1. 10. 80

A siller-haired man
in a broun suit
at Paddy Me'com's
library van

Licht in the een
a swee o the neck
and a lick o the lips
eftir a tellan pint

For ye, maistlie aabodie haed his velua
the crofter and the fairmer

                       (And the laird)

Ye pu'd me back
frae the fur
I wis pleuan
throu society

We c'ud relax a bit
live a bit
wark a bit
no aye chasan
the laitest notion
the auld lear wisna aa wrang
or the auld weys o daean
bit haud on til wir ain ideas

swee, swerve; velua, value; lear, lore; daean, doing; haud, hold

from **Take Five 2006**

At The Edinburgh Book Festival, 2001
for Gillian Slovo

I had no intention of buying a book that day
but realised it would be my only chance
of speaking to Gillian Slovo,
daughter of Joe Slovo, and of Ruth First
killed by the letter bomb in Maputo.

'I greatly admire what your parents did', I said.
But I wonder if she thought,
'Who's that? Is he a Communist?
Why did he say that?
Did he mean what he said?
What did he have in his brief-case?'

This Side Up

James has been packed with anti-Soviet polystyrene chips
And labelled THIS SIDE UP.
Though he travels the world
He hears nothing else.
He will arrive safely.
His neo-liberal views will suffer no displacement.
No anti-capitalist issues will ever reach his ears.
No one will impugn his concern for human rights.
And no daisy-cutters will ever cut *his* daisies.

Susan Weissman - Victor Serge: The Course Is Set On Hope[1]

Verso London and New York 364pp 2001 £22

Suzi you have read every evidence
        interviewed every witness
        detailed every arrest trial sentence assassination suicide
                                            execution

        tracked down every Stalinist agent
        traced every pseudonym
        located every capitulator
        lovingly listed every suspicion
        itemised every failing

After 1918 the Party got almost nothing right anywhere
However one man got almost everything right everywhere

So the course is set on hope
Is it?

---

[1] 'The course is set on hope' is the last line of Serge's poem 'The Constellation of Dead Brothers' written in 1935 in Orenburg and published in *Resistance,* City Light Books, San Francisco, 1989, 34-5.

Escapes And Returns

i.m. James Leslie Mitchell (1901-35)

You grew up here in Arbuthnott under the *code of suppression*
Your *world of multitudinous sense-impressions*
Superimposed with the most narrow and Spartan code of conduct
Ever invented outside Laconia[1]

Trudged 14,000 miles in pursuit of an elementary education
And walked out of the Mackie Academy

Escaped twice to Castlehill Barracks
Rejected when your age was discovered

Escaped to the *Aberdeen Journal*
Joined the Aberdeen Soviet
Admonition had to be given

Escaped to *The Scottish Farmer*
Joined the Left Communist Group of Glasgow
An infantile disorder?

You went off the rails
No, you laid your own line
And you went on laying it
You were never secure

Escaped to the Royal Army Service Corps
Egypt and Iraq, Bethlehem and Jerusalem
Returned at the end of your contract
For five months you could only go out at night
Pointing to the stars and the constellations
Didn't get that ship to Yucatan

Escaped to the Royal Air Force
Married the dark darling in Fulham
Lived in Purley Harrow Hammersmith Welwyn
Wrote seventeen books in seven years

The lexicographer wrote
You lacked an academic training
But now professors write about your books
In Perm, Verona, Rostock, Lyon.

Returned in '24, '25, '29, '31, '32, '33, '34, '35

A great man is dead.
The body is dead, but the spirit will remain.
The work that he has done will remain
And will be an inspiration to the people of Scotland
Now and for many centuries to come.[2]

---

[1] Lewis Grassic Gibbon, *Niger: The Life of Mungo Park,* Edinburgh, 1934, 13.
[2] Ray Mitchell, before the interment of the ashes of James Leslie Mitchell, Arbuthnott, 23 February 1935.

In The Scottish National War Memorial[1]

'... they tell lies about folk they shoot and she'll think I just died like the rest..." - Ewan
 Tavendale to Chae Strachan in *Sunset Song*, Canongate, 238.

Some details are still missing
In these studded red volumes

Nearly every entry follows this order:

Surname
Christian name
Initials for second or more Christian names
Number
Rank
Place of birth
Manner of death
Date of death
Regiment

A small number
Less than forty
Recently entered
Follow an abbreviated version:

Surname
Initial or initials
Number
Rank
Died
Date of death
Regiment

DIED?

They tell lies about folk they shoot
And we'll think you died just like the rest.

---

[1] The names of the Scottish soldiers shot for desertion in the First World War have now
 been entered in the volumes at Edinburgh Castle. One of these may have been the
 model for Ewan Tavendale.

Little Corner Of The World

Little corner of the world
bed with a broken spring
worn waxcloth under it
little corner of the world
      to make love in

Little corner of the world
a jacked-up chair
chilled hands and steel
little corner of the world
      to have pain in

Little corner of the world
man above a desk
green blotter in a case
little corner of the world
      to be cornered in

He Said He Had Read Ignazio Silone

He said he had read Ignazio Silone
And I thought he meant the lot
But when I asked him
He revealed that he had not
Read any
But his friend might have got
One but he wasn't sure what it was
And his friend wasn't sure either

Well, they've got votes too

Shorts

1.	*Revolutionary History*

A permanent Revolution
Or a permanent Opposition?

2.	Middle East Peace

A forced handshake
In Washington

3.	Target

Red lipstick
Fire here

4.	Animal Rights

The reserve champion didn't live to see
His photograph in the paper

5.	Victor Serge

Victor Serge
Is that an overcoat?
Or did he write in Serbo-Croat?

6.	Global Village

In my global village
I only know the names of three living Indonesians
General Suharto
Megawati Sukarnoputri
And Premoedya Ananta Toer

7.   Dalveen Pass, Winter

through a sieving of snow
an earthquake of dykes

8.   you knuckled my window

you knuckled my window
face flushed like the stamp
of a long-lost letter

9.   we are the undershot wheels

we are the undershot wheels
our buckets turned upwards against the clock
no one sees what makes us move

10.   through a corridor of questions

through a corridor of questions
the fan of your headlamps
lit up all my dark trees

11.   you were a course we all passed

you were a course we all passed
I passed for one
though I thought the standard too low

12.   Set In Authority

her well-filled teeth
in her false face

Last Day Of The Year
i.m. Alix Draper

I might never have rung
But someone had withheld their number
And I thought it was you

It wasn't
But you told me
You'd asked them
'How long have I got?'

And they'd looked shifty
And finally mumbled
'Maybe six months'
'Why don't they tell you?'

And they'd maybe try something in the New Year
'But what would that mean?
Longer life? Quality of life?'

'Well', I said, remembering the day,
'All the best'

She had one month

......

And I imagine I hear Alix saying
'It's all very well for you, John, showing your feelings,
You don't know how I got here.'

......

Was Leavis paranoid?
And Lawrence impotent?
What does it matter now?

He Advances Bearing The Weapons Of His Achievement

He advances bearing the weapons of his achievement
The righteous movement he belongs to
The righteous books he has read
The righteous books he has written
The righteous people he recognises
And the righteous people who recognise HIM

Retreat

At The Eventide

Probing with her right hand
The resident defended herself against her wardrobe
One foot inched past the other
Through the long dull tweed
Hung from her middle like a scroll
She said she had never felt so cold

I am not a medical man
And unfortunately only remembered my foreboding later
Know however that at the age of ninety
On her last night on the earth
Miss Sutherland was refused a drink of water
In case she would lie in for breakfast in the morning

Going Walks
for Ginny

We've gone all the good walks -
Henry Moore's headless chicken
Clerk Maxwell's burnt-out house
with the cracked charcoal xylem
The Ponderosa that drenching day
when we lost our way
and kept our tempers

Like laying over photographs
in chronology back to our youth
Let's lay other maps over the matrices
back to the high road with the singing wires
peatstacks and metal boats[1]
Let's go there

---

[1] 'Road-metal' was shaped like an upturned flat-bottomed boat to allow for
   measurement and payment to the stone-breakers.

Confidence Trick

It was only right to match his confidence
                                          I thought
But later a messenger unwittingly revealed
That I had merely added to his power-base
                                        namely, gossip
And now when his friends send
Their unsubtle guided twin-probes
Into my inner space I know where they're coming from.

Arraigned

Suddenly I'm arraigned before my host
I have not read this book
He holds me over the rim of his glasses
How can the conversation go on?
I have not read this book
Is it the only book?

There's a definite delay
An awareness of time passing
Seconds
A minute
Silently he passes
A suspended sentence
And the conversation resumes

Uncollected

Head. Hugh MacDiarmid by William Lamb.
© *Angus Council Cultural Services. From the William Lamb Memorial Studio, Montrose.*

Hugh MacDiarmid Was In Montrose

'Only in 1923 did I learn how to express my thoughts clearly and concisely.'
  - Isaac Babel, 'A brief Autobiography'.

In 1923
Elias Canetti was at school in Frankfurt

Antonio Gramsci left Moscow for Vienna at the end of November

Halldor Laxness was a guest at the Benedictine monastery of Saint
Maurice de Clervaux in the Grand Duchy of Luxemburg

Franz Kafka left Prague to live with Dora Dymant in Berlin

Georg Lukács was in Vienna after the defeat of Béla Kun's government

André Malraux was on an archaelogical expedition in Cambodia

Victor Serge was the correspondent of Inprekorr in Berlin

Ignazio Silone was in prison in Madrid and Barcelona

And Hugh MacDiarmid was in Montrose

MacDiarmid 2000

He was a Communist
He was a eugenist
He was an anarchist
He was a racist
He was a sexist
He was a plagiarist

And after we've deconstructed the monument
It's there

In The Library

There was a silent scholar near me
though many a time I saw him
focussing his microfiches and making notes
like the back of a living bust

yet he had long ears
and once he answered a question
I had addressed to someone else

and once he asked me,
'Has anyone found *The Monmouthshire Labour News*?'[1]
I assured him they had not
and he never spoke to me again.

[1] Hugh MacDiarmid said he worked on *The Monmouthshire Labour News* in Ebbw
    Vale in 1911. Yet no one has found a copy. Perhaps it was too ephemeral to be
    preserved.

Veiled Erotic[1]

nude
in the printshop
only a necklace
leans on a wheel
with curved spokes
a posed mask
in parts

right hand holds
left oxter rests
eyes closed
she dreams
left palm inverted
against her brow
ink print
a signal

her body
a field of shadows
black stripes
curved outlines
nets
- wheel handle
over her pubis

but whould she have driven a tank at Stalingrad?

[1] *Erotique voilée*, 1933, Man Ray. Man Ray was Emmanuel Rudnitsky (1890-1976), artist
and photographer. The editor of *Unmasking Reality*, a book of socialist lectures, put
Man Ray's surrealist image on the cover as a counter to his (the editor's) perception
of the prevailing Soviet view of workers as being only heroes and heroines of
labour.

Für Eine Freundin

Our first bridge was Max Frisch[1]
You did *Homo Faber* in your *gymnasium*
underlined in red
a millimetre under the text
and I told you about *Montauk*
the couple who had arranged
to spend a weekend together
and only one ever
Lynn thirty
Max sixty

I could see you
revolving this idea
and a year later
it was to be a Scottish weekend
with a dram and a peat fire
and porridge for breakfast
in an old house
in a planned village
unlike your town house in Dortmund
I didn't tell you
no one had stayed for six years
still you only found one spider
we did the Jubilee Walk
and went to Caerlaverock
I could see you were thinking
about Easter

We spoke about *lebensraum* and *kristallnacht*
but you didn't talk at all like Hitler

lebensraum living space
kristallnacht the night Jewish businesses were smashed

[1] Max Frisch (1911-1991) published *Homo Faber* in 1957 and *Montauk* in 1975.

At The SECC *(Scottish Exhibition and Conference Centre)*
for a Goth

Cold and clear
side by side
from a hundred miles
and fifty years
apart
I discerned you
in your Marcel Marceau mask
seal's eyelashes
and bat's gloves

we hugged
we were both wearing black coats

15 February 2003

After-Image
for Alice Stilgoe

the window trapezia of the Old Mill showed brochures
and a view of the Nith

the inside wall of the corridor was redbrick
like the universities

with posters for films
and entries of photography

much too narrow for the table
and the 'glass of wine'
served by the butler in red
voices too hectic

before I could speak to you
the officer performed a lightning introduction
of highlights

later I realised Modigliani had painted you

Alice Stilgoe is film officer at the Robert Burns Centre in the Old Mill, Dumfries. The
'officer' in the poem was then Literature Development Officer with Dumfries and
Galloway Arts Association.

Twice Met

Once before you had passed
on George Fourth Bridge
a year ago
almost subliminally.

Your face -
with the flat lump still spreading
all over one side
which you cover with white flour

and the lesser side –
blanched shrunk skin over bone
below a bird's eye.

Now with two clung plastic bags
you still edge one foot past the other

and for how long?

Leaving Edinburgh University Library Special Collections

Friday afternoon at the Library
I finish an hour early
with several coats of tiredness absorbed
and return to the outside world
of smokers, railings, yellow hats
go down the pebble-dashed steps
over the cuboid cobbles of George Square
and along the left side of the white stick
for cyclists spinning into the Meadows
and past the red-doored Bedlam
with the fiery hinges

I'm in two minds
I want to go home
and I want to see Bruna at the Elephant House
if she's there

and she is there
between the galley
and the tables
in her informal uniform
blue bandana in her hair

then I go for the train

Iranian Woman In George Street, Edinburgh
at the time of John Major's Presidency of the E.U., December, 1992.

A woman in black holds a black book
in the shelter of shops
on the south side of George Street
She beckons to me
and turns over the pages
the heads of the dead in Iran
over a thousand last year
the hanged, the beaten
the petitions, the signatures
the sponsors

All day, clashes and sprays of rain
Drops dilate the laminated pages
It's not a night for sympathy
It's half dark
We're strangers
Knocks of passers' feet
and hiss of wet wheels
I lose some of her good English
She's been there for eight hours

Christmas cake letters in twelve languages
Windows cut out like turnip lanterns
Lights split into compass points
And round the corner the Castle
with its drum of three courses
the tones
the stones

To Pollokshaws West
à Béatrice

'It was a lovely day' we said
I brought the map and you checked the train
To Pollokshaws West on the trail of John MacLean
'FAMOUS PIONEER OF WORKING-CLASS EDUCATION
HE FORGED THE SCOTTISH LINK IN THE GOLDEN CHAIN OF WORLD
SOCIALISM'
The legend incised on the smoothed area of the hewn pillar
All by himself? And *has* it been forged?

What are the odd couple doing? –
The young student with her shoulder bag
The old scholar with his briefcase –
Thought the workers on the demolition site
At the pyramid of tilting boards and stour

Our last day
We sat on the green herring-bone perforations
17.30 ON TIME
But what's the platform?
The info fades and reappears
Then there were only four minutes left
And the surge to Platform 5

Gordon Brown's Schooldays

'[The Rector] said if there were any boys who were desperate to
watch the [Italy v. Scotland] game, they should come to his office after
assembly to discuss it. Some of the boys went round, thinking the
headmaster might put a TV in one of the classrooms. Instead, he got
them in one by one, gave them a good belting, and told them if they
tried to play truant that afternoon, they'd get another belting every day
for a month.'
- Rosamond Hutt, *The Herald*, 08.12.08

So they walked into the trap
A discussion
The belt

How to find words for
The warped use of language
Not yet unveiled in S3

The language of power
The language of terror

A thrashing for thinking

May *his* hands burn in hell

Nightmare

'I had taken early retirement
But went back to work temporarily immediately
Which became permanently

I hope the Records of Work aren't called in
I haven't written mine for a year
It would be almost impossible to catch up in a night
Maybe they're not needed now
Perhaps a different philosophy is in place
And everyone has to defer to it
But why hadn't I kept mine after all the hassle?'

In Victoria Street

In a brace of the brackets
of my dark descending street
of doors, garages and arches
one only remembers another time
comes up the street
and calls my name clearly
outside my lit red blind
I don't know who
I open the door
She steps forward
cheeks red with cold
under her white inverted hat

Christmas 2006

In St David's Street

We edged across the gap to meet
along the street

You recognised your neighbours
quietly and efficiently

But I held back civil and restrained
and gave them no time

I wanted to speak to you
and you to speak to me

Snaps

For Tatiana

You tripped to Venice
with bangles and shoulder bag
posed beside the Kama
with Volga for tributary
and now you stand among the cubes
of the Third Perm International Ice Figures Festival
your hat a judge's beehive -
pity about the Coca-Cola tent

Laird And Tall Woman On A Bench On Perth Railway Station

the laird thinning on top
from an aerial view
wearing long Johns trousers
in clean green wellies
fresh from mock byre mucking
reading *The Times*

tall woman leaning on his shoulder
overlooking his head
laird's bonnet laid on her curls
not reading *The Times*

together they move off to the business class

Whim

A hint in your voice
on the phone
after not meeting for months
'It's a bright morning'

I didn't respond
needing to be part of a plan
not a whim

Like an auctioneer
you waited a second
for my bid
and then banged your gavel
and I was 'out'
someone else was higher

Power Of The Medium

It was almost the close of play in Australia
the first tour after the War
which had taken such an enormous chunk
out of these players' careers
seven years
as it did to so many

But they were still there:
Hutton and Washbrook
Edrich and Compton
Hammond and Yardley
Gibb and Voce and Wright
and Compton made a century in each innings in Adelaide
147 and 103*

And I was listening
beside the open hearth
waiting to go on the school bus
fifteen miles along the north coast to Thurso

Acknowledgements

Grateful acknowledgement is made to the following publications:

East Sutherland
East Sutherland and other poems. Reidhmásach Press © John Manson, 1985.
Some of the poems first appeared in Akros, Calgacus, Catalyst, Cencrastus,
Fireweed, The Glasgow Herald, *Poems of the Scottish Hills* (Aberdeen
University Press), Schools Bulletin (Dumfries and Galloway Regional Council),
Scotia Review, Scottish Marxist, *Scottish Poetry 5, 6* (Edinburgh University
Press), The John MacLean Society Journal, *Three Poems* (Castlelaw Press,
1972), United Scotsman, and Weighbauk.

Malevich in Edinburgh
Malevich in Edinburgh. Volume Nine in the Galloway Poets series.
ISBN 1 901913 08 7, Markings Publications, Kirkcudbright, 1997.
Some of the poems were first published in Akros, Akros Verse 1965-82,
Catalyst, Lallans, Markings, *Norman MacCaig A Celebration* (Chapman
Publishing, 1995), Scotia Rampant, Scotia Review, Southfields, Spectrum, *The
New Makars* (Mercat Press, 1991), *With Both Feet Off The Ground* (Dumfries
and Galloway Libraries, Information and Archives, 1993) and $Zed_2 0$.

Pleuan first appeared, with Rosalie Loveday's illustration, as *Caithness
Ploughing 1940* in Catalyst, Winter 1968.
Ena's and *Yir Brither Wis Lost At Sea* also later appeared in Pulteney Pressings
(Wick, 2008, 2009).

Take Five 06
Take Five 06 ISBN: 1 904886 36 1, Shoestring Press, Nottingham, 2006.
Some of the poems first appeared in *Casablanca Diary* (1995), Fireweed,
Poetry Scotland (Callander), *The Sound of Our Voices* (Dumfries and Galloway
Libraries, Information and Archives, 1999), *Voices of Dissent* and West Coast
Magazine.

Uncollected
A number of these poems has previously appeared in print in Epoch (Issue
9, Montrose, 1996), *For Angus* (Los Poetry Press, 2009), Groundswell (2000),
Markings (Issues 20-21: Kirkcudbright, 2005 and 30: Gatehouse of Fleet,
2010), The Herald (Glasgow), *Poetry on the Bus* (Dumfries and Galloway Arts
Association, 2004) and Poetry Scotland (Callander).

About the Author

John Manson was born in 1932 in Caithness where his parents were crofters. In his early twenties his mother and he moved to a croft in Sutherland, the county from which his great-grandmother had been cleared.

He has also lived in Aberdeen and Aberdeenshire, Motherwell, Roxburghshire, Cumbria, Edinburgh, Fife, and for 37 years in Galloway. John's working life has been spent in crofting, reading/writing and teaching.

Since early retirement he has focussed on research on Scottish authors of the 1930s, mainly Hugh MacDiarmid, Lewis Grassic Gibbon and James Barke, as well as on translation of prose and poetry into English and of poetry into Scots.

His publications include co-editorship with David Craig of the first Penguin paperback edition of Hugh MacDiarmid's *Selected Poems* (1970); co-editorship of *The Revolutionary Art of the Future: Rediscovered Poems by Hugh MacDiarmid*, with Dorian Grieve and Alan Riach (Carcanet Press, 2003). He selected and edited *Dear Grieve: Letters to Hugh MacDiarmid* (Kennedy and Boyd, 2011).

CPSIA information can be obtained at www.ICGtesting.com
Printed in the USA
LVOW12s2126051213

364128LV00013B/160/P